With Wakened Hands

With Wakened Hands

Furniture by James Krenov and Students

Seth Janofsky, Principal Photographer

Cambium Press · Bethel/Linden Publishing · Fresno

With Wakened Hands

© 2000 by James Krenov

ISBN: Hardcover 1-892836-07-6
       Paperback 1-892836-06-8

First printing: October 2000
Printed in Hong Kong

Published jointly by
   Cambium Press
   P.O. Box 909
   Bethel, CT 06801
   800-238-7724, fax 203-778-2785
   www.cambiumbooks.com

   Linden Publishing, Inc.
   336 West Bedford · Suite 107
   Fresno, California 93711
   800-345-4447
   www.lindenpub.com

Library of Congress
Cataloging-in-Publication Data
Krenov, James
     With wakened hands / furniture by James Krenov and students ; with photographs by
Seth Janofsky.
        p. cm.
     Includes index.
     ISBN 1-892836-07-6 -- ISBN 1-892836-06-8 (paper)
     1. Furniture Making. 2. Furniture Design. I. Janofsky, Seth, 1956- II. Title.

TT194 .K74 2000
684.1'04--dc21

                                                        00-023601

Acknowledgments

The need to build a bridge between my students and the people who will appreciate their work has been in my mind for a very long time—even before the beginning of the school. Such thoughts were set aside for a time, but not from procrastination or a lack of means. As soon as you start thinking of writing a book, resources become important. You must have a realistic approach to funding and publishing. I did my other books without any financial foundation whatsoever—with no advances from the publisher or from anyone else.

Before starting this book, I fumbled, postponed, and wondered how to do it until a gentleman by the name of Robert W. Bruce, III, visited the shop along with his wife. We chatted. Mr. Bruce mentioned that he had seen my work and even acquired a bit of it, and I in turn told him about my wish—indeed my need—to do one last thing on the planet. I told him I needed to create a book about the school, the students, and their work. Mr. Bruce generously made a donation, and suddenly this book became a possibility.

Of course, I could go on and on thanking any number of people—my colleagues, my students, and people who have encouraged me. But I feel that it would be better to simply say that there are a great number of persons who have contributed their feelings, opinions, and photography to the making of this book. It is not really to my credit. I don't consider it my book; I look upon it as our book.

In the actual doing of the book, my editor, Aimé Fraser, played a role with her patience and perseverance. And as in the case of all the writing I have ever done, my wife, Britta, has been behind me with humor and grace and patience when it was tough going, and when it was good. She is always there. Always.

D. H. Lawrence wrote a short story about a meeting between two strangers high in the mountains of Switzerland. The two men sat together looking out over the world, and after a time they parted, each going his own way. The story ends something like this: "Though I have lost his address and forgotten his name, my friend is my friend forever."

—*James Krenov, February 2000*

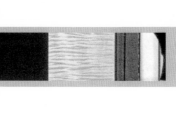 # Contents

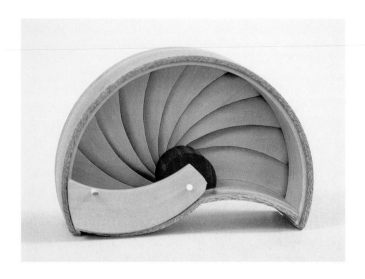

Foreword

Rarely in the history of craft has a name been so widely recognized or so greatly respected. Master craftsman, educator, and tireless apostle of a uniquely personal and spiritual style of woodworking, James Krenov is probably the most influential woodworker of the twentieth century in terms of the sheer number of craftspeople whose work and sensibilities he has affected.

For most woodworkers and craft aficionados, the mention of Krenov brings to mind the furniture idioms for which he is famous—tall "chest-on-stand" pieces with gracefully curving legs and bowed fronts, understated wall cabinets, precious drawers and fittings, hand-carved latches and pulls, simple finishes, and lyrical marquetry and parquetry patterns executed to near perfection—each piece a *tour de force* of line, form, texture, and detail. But, Krenov's greatest legacy will likely prove to be the unique awareness he has brought to writing about the craft of woodworking: a profound sensitivity to personal feelings and attitude, to tools as an extension of the mind and hand, and to the infinite possibilities inherent in wood itself.

Krenov's woodworking philosophy came to public attention in his first three books—*A Cabinetmaker's Notebook* (1975), *The Fine Art of Cabinetmaking* (1977), and *The Impractical Cabinetmaker* (1979). In them, he wrote about woodworking in a refreshing new way, about the delightful subtleties of wood and the personal satisfaction that results from the craftsman's willingness to become involved physically, intellectually, and emotionally with the tools and the materials of the craft.

This romantic approach to craftsmanship resonated deeply within the growing ranks of young people who had turned to craft work in the late 1960s and early 1970s. They were particularly receptive to Krenov's rejection of the culture's prevailing production mentality, which he blamed for

This page:
Krenov opens one of his cabinets.

Opposite page:
Krenov at his bench, circa 1993.

"engineer art"—lifeless design motivated primarily by manufacturing expediency.

The immense popularity of Krenov's books placed him squarely among those at the forefront of a modern craft renaissance that has continued to grow and flourish in the U.S. for the last quarter-century.

In the intervening years, Krenov has occupied himself with teaching and furniture making. The school he founded in 1981 at The College of the Redwoods, in Fort Bragg, CA, has become a haven for ambitious and talented students of all ages from around the world, united by their passion for fine craftsmanship and their adulation of this master and his philosophy.

Krenov's teaching style, consistent with his philosophy of personal sensitivity as the basis for craft, is almost Zen-like in its encouragement of introspection and self-inquiry as the source of growth and enlightenment. In his quick, self-effacing, and sometimes impish way, he delivers his critiques in the form of questions and oblique suggestions, which convey his point without becoming too didactic. The objective, after all, is for the students to find the solutions from within themselves. Judging from the remarkable quality of the students' work (which you will see for yourself in this book), Krenov's method seems to be working quite well.

The biggest challenge for graduates of Krenov's program is to apply their newly acquired skills in the real world. As the title of his third book (*The Impractical Cabinetmaker*) implies, Krenov is well aware that his meticulous approach to woodworking is time-consuming and costly, which is why his teachings are aimed primarily at "amateurs in the true sense of the word" who don't need to make a living at it. Those students who hope to survive as professional woodworkers must find the galleries and patrons who are willing to pay for such refined work—a daunting task for many, but one that promises to become easier as new ways are devised to raise the public's awareness and appreciation of high craft.

Today, at 80 years of age, Jim Krenov is still at the top of his game. He plays tennis regularly, and spends much of his time doing the things he loves best: working wood and sharing his wealth of experience with people who admire and respect him. We should all be so fortunate.

I think you'll find this book to be a fitting tribute to Krenov and an enlightening overview of his distinguished career, his abiding philosophy, and his most important legacy—the spirit of craftsmanship that he has now successfully passed along to two generations of woodworkers.

—Ellis Walentine, December 1999

Section *1*: Workmanship

· The Timeless Quest

Things men have made with wakened hands, and put soft life into
Are awake through years with transferred touch and go on glowing
For long years.
And for this reason, some old things are lovely
Warm still with the life of forgotten men who made them.

—D. H. Lawrence

The Timeless Quest

This is about the many craftsmen who have studied at The College of the Redwoods in Fort Bragg, CA, during the last 20 years. Although they are now scattered throughout America and other parts of the world, they share a common quest: the persistent desire to know their craft, do their best, and express their true selves in the work. They have undertaken a constant and often perilous search for excellence.

In the past, craftsmen working in the traditional way sought the same things. In these times of ever increasing self-assertion, when people seek the new, the garish, and the striking, the craftsman's timeless quest is nearly forgotten.

Our students continue the quest for excellence—dangerously at times, and often at great sacrifice. But they are on the verge of achieving their primary aim: making a living by making fine things and through the making finding happiness.

This quest for excellence, though it has always existed, got new energy during the 1970s when there was a re-evaluation, a revolt even, against unhappiness in work and dullness in life. During and after the Vietnam War, in many places around the world this re-evaluation resulted in people wanting to change the direction of their lives. They sought to be less dependent on gadgets and counting the boss's money. They wanted to live life in a happier, more generous, and warmer emotional climate.

I experienced this in Sweden. After receiving a very thorough and traditional education in cabinetmaking, I worked alone in my little shop for many years. The climate was congenial to the kind of work I did—work that was unpretentious and which involved all of myself in an attempt to consistently express something that was scarcely tangible at times. It emerged now and then, and over time my work began to be recognized and appreciated by a few people.

More through chance than anything else, I

Overleaf:
Intimacy of skills is more important than mere mechanics.

This page:
The wood a craftsman works must excite and energize him.

Opposite page:
Students at The College of the Redwoods share a common goal: to do their best and express their true selves in the work.

received invitations to return to America and teach at various universities. As a result of this, I was asked if I would write a book, and thanks to the persistence of my friend Craig McArt, *A Cabinetmaker's Notebook* was published in 1976.

The book changed not only my life, but the lives of many of the people who read it. Readers were delighted to learn of a woodworker who, though not a great success himself, would not give up, and who persistently wanted to be himself in his work. I received letters from people far and wide, both thanking me and asking me to write even more about our craft. I wrote more books, continued my teaching, and in time I was offered the chance to establish a school with The College of The Redwoods in Fort Bragg. I accepted for several reasons. One of the most important was that it is a community college.

Before the offer came, I had visited quite a few universities and colleges, most of which were privately endowed schools where it cost a student ten to twenty thousand dollars just to walk through the door. Here was a chance to teach in a place that was much more accessible in the financial sense. The college is practically free for Californians, and the out-of-state tuition is less than one quarter of what it costs to attend one of those other institutions.

In principle, this kind of education should be accessible to all, in the way we are. The only requirements are rudimentary hand skills and some knowledge of the craft. Choosing students as we do, we get a great variety of talents, aptitudes, and experiences. We tune in to this and adapt our teaching to the student, regardless of how much skill he or she possesses.

I say he or she because from the very beginning we have had women here, usually two or three, but at times more. We have been forerunners in accepting women into woodworking and cabinetmaking and I am proud of that.

The school has become a home for a growing number of craftsmen who continue to persevere in their quest for refinement. For the most part they are surviving and doing unquestionably excellent work. Yet there seems to me to be a grave lack of appreciation for this kind of work. These craftsmen and women need appreciation to encourage them as they continue along their chosen path. I

have done my best to help them, but was often frustrated by lack of means.

This work we do is low-key and unpretentious, and yet in its essence very demanding. It is the synthesis of knowledge and intuition. It also requires a certain feeling for wood, as well as a respect for and curiosity about it. Wood is a living material, quite unforgiving, and sometimes very elusive. It takes for granted that we are sensitive in hand and eye and that our whole being—our intuition, our sense of proportion, line, and detail—is finely tuned yet always modest.

Modesty in craftsmen is always a perilous quality, very vulnerable in these times of computerized vision, TV advertisements, and the worn-out word "quality." Rather than use that confusing word, I find that it is better to talk of workmanship, which is the sum total of the skills and sensitivities of the craftsman. This pursuit of excellence, of workmanship, draws us to attend to the details and possibilities in the work.

The intimacy of the process that defines workmanship is the result of sensitivity of tool and eye and hand—of all of one's senses. It is not driven by ego, but rather by a sincere and lasting desire to do one's best and to be proud of what one has done. There is integrity in this.

The output of such craftsmen is, of necessity, higher in quality, but they create fewer pieces. As a result, the public that appreciates such quiet work is small. But the appreciation we enjoy is genuine, especially in Europe. The pace there is slower and there is more continuity. Historically craftsmen have enjoyed more respect there than they do in the United States. But the number of these fine,

This page:
Krenov at work in the benchroom.

Opposite page:
Cabinet on a stand, James Krenov.
Kwila, pear wood, and olive. 4 ft. 3 in. high, 18 in. wide, 12 in. deep. The showcase section is fairly shallow. The stand seemed empty; it needed visual help, hence the bracing.

dedicated craftsmen who are making great sacrifices to survive is slowly increasing. Our school is evidence of this.

My goal for this book is to bring this refined work to the attention of the public. While it is not "Art Furniture," surely artistry is expressed in every turn. The furniture is functional, and finely crafted in ways that make the object a pleasure to use and to pass on to others.

I have a letter somewhere from a museum curator who says that our graduates should have no trouble at all surviving and finding an appreciative audience for their work. I'm sure the lady means what she says, but judging by my experience, it may be a bit of wishful thinking. She acknowledges that museum curators, gallery people, and interior decorators should make more of an effort to understand this particular kind of work in addition to the jazzy, showy things that claim most of their attention. It is my hope that—with the help of this book, our shows, and other events—we will succeed in achieving a greater degree of success. We want to make contact with the people for whom this kind of work will be a pleasure to follow, to observe, and to live with. That is my last task on the planet and the reason for writing this book.

I never became a member of the club of superstar craftsmen, though I have rubbed elbows with many of them. I have a piece in the Philadelphia Museum of Art, which makes me happy, but the rest of my public life as a craftsman has been quiet. I don't want to drink cocktails and scratch somebody's back or have my own back scratched. It's not necessary.

Not being mainstream and not being recognized has never really bothered me. At the same time I must admit that the echoes from the books have pleased me. People seem to admire what I do. I get my small share of praise and admiration. So everything is just fine. I don't have a score to settle, or a bone to pick.

I have wonderful students who often become friends. I continue to make pieces, and somehow they quietly find their way to the people who seem to appreciate them—people who call me up later and say, "You know, that piece of yours that we got, the cabinet? We really like it. It warms us. We show it to our friends and tell them how you made it."

As a quiet craftsman, my work has been low key and fairly simple, and I have always leaned heavily on wood, and the work of my hands and my eyes relating to that wood.

I have a little hideout in one far corner of the building. There is a sign on the door that says, "Please knock." There's a great deal of knocking, which I enjoy. There I am tucked in the corner, an old guy, and I am still needed.

That knock on the door is often made by somebody who wants to ask me something. Usually he or she wants to take me out to the shop, show me a piece of work, and ask me to help. I'm not on the scrap heap. I appreciate very much that the college is allowing me to stay, and I intend to stay as long as I am clear-headed and physically capable. When I get certain signals I will ride away into the sunset.

I work and I make cabinets. I no longer acquire wood that is not dry. Even if it is wonderful wood, if it's wet or freshly sawn and wet, I pass it up. Who knows if I'll be around the three years it takes to dry? I've got a little bit of wood left, and there is more out in the shop, so I'm all right.

I work fairly well, seeing how I have to overcome the arthritis in my right hand. I am able to work in a way that pleases me, that fills me with a purpose and with a certain secret satisfaction I enjoy sharing with my students. They like to see me doing it and not just talking about it. These last few years I have found a new freedom to experiment and do things I have never before dared.

On days when I do not have to teach and the weather is fairly good, I go with my wife, Britta, to the cliffs along the shore. We watch the pelicans, seagulls, pipers, and seals on the rocks, and we look out at the wide Pacific. When there is a heavy surf running and an easterly wind, we stand there watching the great waves uncurl for a mile or more toward Glass Beach and the entrance to Noyo Harbor. As the waves break in slow motion, the wind takes the foam from the crest and blows it back to sea, like a scarf unfurling. Now and then, if the sun peeks through among the clouds, then the fine spray at the tops of the waves becomes fragments of a rainbow. Britta and I hold hands as we look at the great ocean before us and breathe a sigh.

I stand at the edge of the wide world
And think till fame and love to nothingness do sink.

— *John Donne*

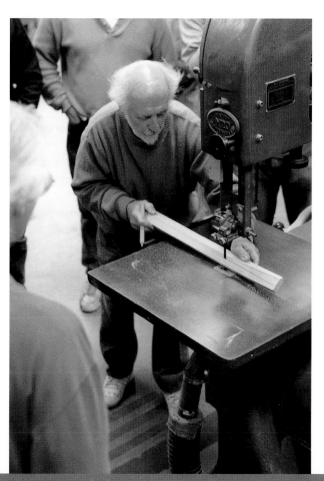

Section 2: Teaching

We tell the students that if they worry less, concentrate more, and above all relax, they're going to be all right....

The School

Students come to our school with different levels of skills and abilities. Some have a very fine sense of design, proportion, line, and detail, but the real doing of cabinetmaking comes hard to them. They may have certain difficulties organizing their work, keeping it moving, and avoiding simple errors. Those are the errors that embarrass and set one back, not only physically but mentally.

We work hard with these students, and at the end of about two months we have gone through the alphabet. We've talked about wood and its charms and frustrations, and we've covered all the traditional hand tools and how to use them with the best possible result and the least amount of effort.

Then comes the first project, and we try to encourage students to hold back and keep within the limits of what they have learned. Even at this point, there is still a variety of levels and results. But we avoid calamities; we avoid the unsuccessful piece.

As the year progresses, students challenge themselves more, and we work even harder to keep them out of trouble and help them every way we can. By this time we're studying veneering, which is easily misunderstood. Something veneered, like a cabinet or a table, should be different in character from something made in solid wood.

The year goes on, and we watch the students as they progress, and we prepare ourselves for the time when we will be allowing five or six of them to stay a second year. This is a very difficult time, and a terrible strain on those of us who must make the choice. Often more students would like to stay than the agreement with the college allows us to keep. We do our best and so do they, and some who aren't chosen know that if they wait for a year or so we can give them another chance to stay on.

At the end of the year we have the major student

Overleaf:
Left: Krenov's workplace in the back corner. Don't forget to knock!
Right: The experienced craftsman knows by looking at a plank just how it should be cut to yield a surface that contains a certain curve of grain or change in color.

This page:
The College of the Redwoods Fine Woodworking Program staff. From left: James Krenov, Michael Burns, Jim Budlong, and David Welter.

Opposite page:
The benchroom.

show. It is an occasion of intense feelings. The year is being summarized, we are getting ready to part with some of these people, and they are presenting themselves and their work to the public.

We do not judge the pieces in the art school manner. I have experienced my share of these art-oriented critiques and have found that they can be quite vicious and destructive. At our school, everyone gathers around the piece with some coffee and sweets, and we listen to the builders' narratives of how each piece was done and how they feel about it. Students make friendly comments that are well meant even if they seem mildly critical, and these presentations result in encouragement rather than in destructive put downs that breed self-doubt and negative feelings.

Here at the school we have a reverence for the past, but we do not dwell in it. On the other hand, we are not re-inventing woodworking. We are simply continuing in the steps of craftsmen who did fine things and then passed away, while the things themselves lived on. We speak here not only of woodworking, but of music, sculpture, literature, and of people across time who have done wonderful things and left us inspiring works. These efforts

nourish a craftsman working alone with only a faint hope of appreciation. And though of late I am not lacking in appreciation, I still feel a deep desire to share some of that inspiration and see it passed on to my students.

Teaching, as I see it, is sharing. The more adventures and emotions you've discovered and experienced as a craftsman and as a person, the more you have to share. I enjoy sharing gentle shapes, forms, friendly edges, wood, and its living qualities without demanding anything of my students.

The way we teach is very direct and relaxing. We don't go through the old-fashioned disciplines in the old-fashioned way. We don't tell people that it is going to take them years to learn to do something half as well as I or my colleagues can do it. We go directly to the fact that if you worry less, concentrate more, and above all relax, you'll be all right.

Almost all the students who apply to our school are familiar with my books, which represent our approach to the craft, and have responded positively to their spirit. This results in a group that is relaxed, and good to one another. They share their work rather than protect it. I have visited universi-

9

This page:
Krenov and Ted Hawke, 1984.

Opposite page:
Above: There isn't the competitiveness here such as we see elsewhere. People push themselves to get the knowledge and *do* things.
Below: Teaching is sharing.

ties and colleges where there is an ego-driven competition. It is not always wholesome, and it can be destructive.

We don't have that. My colleagues Michael Burns, Jim Budlong, David Welter, and I have a simple, straightforward approach. We start by talking about wood and tools, but we always keep in focus the sensitivities and discoveries—the things that craftsmen can use and build upon to make the craft their own. This fosters a friendly competitiveness. People push themselves to get knowledge and accomplish things. Sometimes we must chase them home in the evening, and they're back early in the morning to remind us of their presence.

During these last years, we've had an increased sense of what you might call independence. Students at a certain point may say, "I'm going out on my own. I want to make this, and I hope you don't object." There are always concerns about the workmanship of putting a piece together, but the most important question is always *"Is it worth doing?"* Is it really worth the time and the effort and the emotion of creating it? So we talk about it. We come to an agreement that there are little dangers, that the piece or the technique might be experimental, but it won't be weird or ugly. We agree that it is worth doing.

I am certainly an influence on the students, just as any teacher with a strong sense of direction has an influence. But I do not shape people. Much of the work from our school reflects a certain spirit and sensitivity, an intimacy in the process of working with wood, but not necessarily the same proportions or design. Only rarely does a student ask if he or she can make a version of something I have done.

There is a delicate balance between shaping students' sensibilities and letting them find their own way. On one hand, you want the work coming from the school to reflect the values that you teach and to have a certain look and feel that is recognizable. People see it in the curves, form, and in the work. It has balance, and is soft without being mushy. At its best our work is pleasing and undemanding to the eye.

Over the last few years especially, people have begun to edge away from that recognizable quality. They diverge from what might be considered my sense of aesthetics. Why has this happened? At

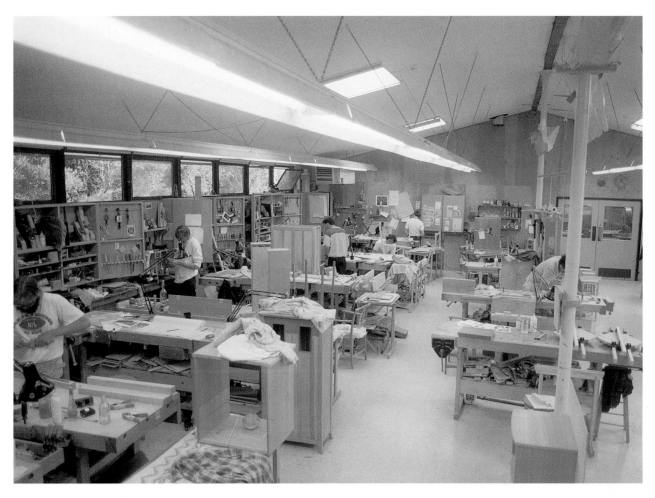

what point do you let go and let the student do something aesthetically unpleasing?

That's a crucial question. Being as old as I am, and having been here as long as I have, I'm starting to see the beginning of a transition. Someday the school will run itself. I am gradually nearing the time when there will be even fewer demands made on me. I won't be around; other people will. I sometimes don't have the determination and energy to be the only one who points out that something won't work, that it won't sing. I don't want the school to lose sight of the things we have taught. We get a few people every year who want more freedom and who don't accept what we stand for at all. They just want a place to work. There's nothing bad about that, but I don't want to see the school becoming a mere trade school for woodworking.

We have a long list by the telephone with the address and phone number of every student who has ever gone to our school. Students call often—not with an SOS, but just to tell us they are all right. They let us know that they look back on their time here with pride, humor, and gratitude. Life is good because I know they are all right.

Along with my pride that we have done our best for each and every student, I worry a great deal about their futures. I *know* some of the difficulties a quiet craftsman will encounter. And they will continue to be difficulties until more people realize the worth of this work, its emotional content, and its intrinsic value .

Intimacy of Skills

This page and opposite:
Showcase cabinet on stand, René Almon.
59 in. high, 22 in. wide, 12 in. deep. European cherry, and teak. Shellac, polish, and wax finish.

"I've worked as a boat builder and a kitchen cabinet maker, but until I went to the school all of my work was pretty boxy. I wanted to change that. One day, during my second year at the school, I was looking through one of the books. I saw a picture of one of Jim's cabinets. I just loved those legs. The top of this cabinet was my idea, but the legs were inspired by Jim's work. About the door panels: I cut into that plank of European cherry and found what some people might have thought was a flaw. It had a knot, but the way the grain came out of it was just beautiful. Some people would have just cut the knot off, but I made it part of my design."

—*René Almon*

Most of the ease and enjoyment of woodworking comes through simple processes that require harmony, both mentally and physically. You have to focus on the work and ask yourself questions. For instance, if you are not sharpening well, it is probably an unnatural movement in your hands or arms that is the problem. It is attention to these seemingly insignificant things that is the beginning of habit. It's the first link in a long chain that gradually becomes a natural way of working. You no longer worry about the physical aspects of a tool but about what you're going to do with it. You're thinking about how it's going to feel and how the result will look.

While these fundamental skills are vital and require desire and patience to learn, the central thing is the flexibility or intimacy of a craftsman's skills. It's knowing when precisely square is crucial, and when it is not. There is something we call flexible accuracy—straight, and yet alive. Doing good work can be a strain, but don't immobilize yourself worrying too much about it.

Between the engineer and the poet there is a distance measured only by the quiet voice of intuition.

Years ago I read and clipped a paragraph that sums this up. I am no longer able to remember the source, but it is about Stanley Doubtfire, an English engraver and luthier. "Over the years he methodically discovered many of the secrets of instrument making. Despite practical skill, knowledge of techniques, and familiarity with materials, he found that chance, sheer chance, could still play a feckless part in the quality of the finished instrument. One could make judgements from experience yet always, and it seemed at every stage, there were intangible

factors that could affect the final outcome. And the haunting uncertainty was that you did not know, for sure, where or when, or even if, they had occurred. The challenge was always to produce the perfect instrument."

There is a stage at which many of us are frustrated because our skills aren't up to our expectations. We're not completely in control. It is important at those times not to challenge yourself too far beyond your abilities.

I think it's important before starting a piece to sit down and talk about not only how you are going to build it, but how you are going to feel while building it. You want to do things that will make you happy.

Keep away from intimidation. Don't allow yourself to get in over your head. Sometimes it's hard to know the depth of the water. We talk about the technical aspects, and I ask, "How do you feel about doing this particular kind of work? This is a piece demanding tremendous accuracy; that other is a piece that is relaxed and casual. If you do it this way, the joinery doesn't have to be perfect." Often the student will be relieved to hear this because he or she didn't want to get trapped in close inhuman measurements and accurate joints. I'm not encouraging sloppy workmanship, ever. But relax, please.

Relating to tools is not quite like Gertrude Stein said about the rose. A chisel is a chisel is a chisel. But a chisel can be honed, sharpened, and used in different ways for different purposes. A chisel is not merely a tool, it is an instrument. And with that instrument you can enjoy your work.

This page:
Display cabinet, Bill Merikallio.

Opposite page:
Detail of carved Douglas fir panel in a secretaire by Austin Meinert.

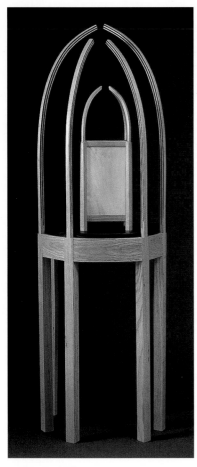

This page:
"Shelter," Horschel Matka Weiss. Ash, cocobolo, Swiss pear, and an unidentified yellow wood. 61 in. high, 19.5 in. wide, 14.5 in. deep. Made after graduation from The College of the Redwoods, this piece is intended to display a single item on an adjustable self within the "house."

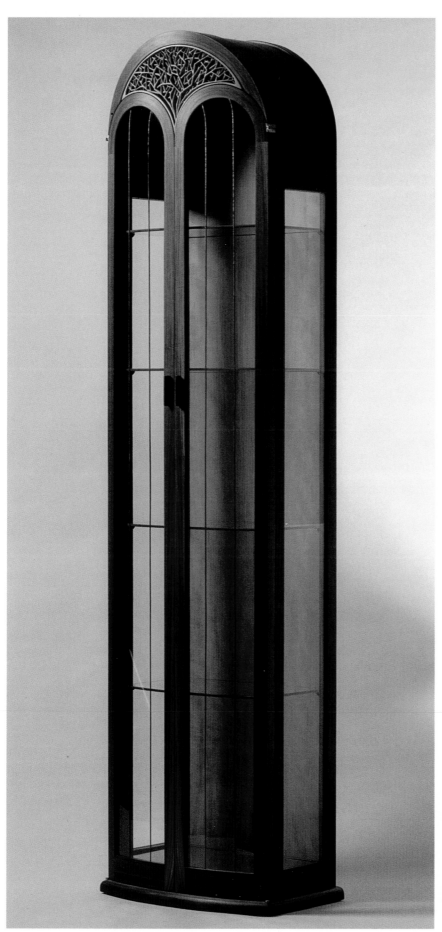

This page:
Tall showcase, Brian Newell.
Pao ferro, pear. 70 in. high,
15 in. wide, 8 in. deep.
Copper foil joints in the glass,
pierced carving.

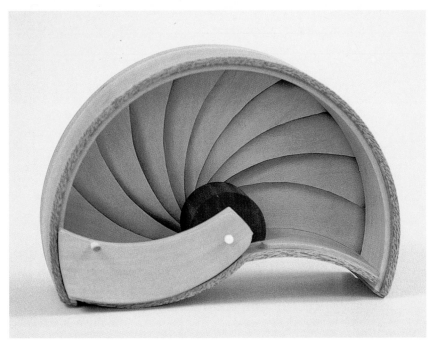

This page:
"Feathers," Armin Driver. Holly, sycamore, ebony, frost-killed Fort Bragg sandalwood, and tagua nut. 3.5 in. high, 8.5 in. wide, 5.5 in. deep. A few people have a talent for design that combines precision with a sense of balance and rhythm.

"The inspiration for this piece was my grandmother's fan. People in my native India still use wooden fans in the warm climate. The way in which the fan folded made me think it would be interesting to make a box that used the same mechanism."
—Armin Driver

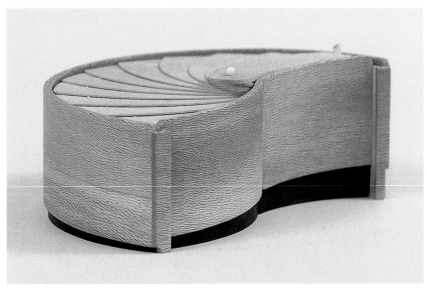

This page:
Box, Brian Newell.
15 in. high, 15 in. wide, 6 in. deep.
Applewood and East Indian rosewood.

"After 20 years working with wood, I'm still doing battle with simplicity. The roots are deep; where I grew up in Michigan, a piece of furniture without some form of swirling foliage stamped into it was virtually invisible. Everywhere was counterfeit rococo and chair legs turned with a thousand bumps. I live in Japan now, a country that has managed over several centuries to make the square look good."
—Brian Newell

When we first started, there was quite a bit of skepticism about us, and even some irritation, in the woodworking community. Magazines sometimes spoke of us as being way out in left field, and said that our students would be shocked when they left us for the "real world." Twenty years later, I must say that a lot of them have discovered a "real world" where they are able to quietly go about their work. They live the life that they have chosen, with its inherent hazards, setbacks, and deep secret satisfactions.

Skeptics are surprised at the high percentage of our students who are still craftsmen and getting along in the world. A few of them are very well known craftsmen doing beautifully. Some are working for others in high-end furniture shops making very expensive things for very rich people. These former students often end up being given the most difficult work in the shop because they are so skilled and sensitive. Others are working quietly, as I said, by themselves, surviving and getting along and making friends, and working their way from one modest commission to the next. On the whole, the apprehension that I felt in those first years, when we were bombarded with criticism, is gone. So is the criticism. We have slowly but surely become known as a good school for a certain type of person with a certain kind of aspiration.

In the beginning there was the assumption that I create, educate, and encourage little Krenovs—that the student work is somewhat cramped or at least affected by me. Yes, I am an influence, but I do not shape people. We encourage our students to work with a spirit of sensitivity and intimacy in the process of working with wood, but we don't dictate the proportions, the design, or even the subject.

The majority of our students are in a one-year program, but we have been given permission by the College to keep six people by mutual agreement for

This page and opposite:
Interior, Ross Day.
Mahogany and cherry. Lacquer varnish finish.
Ross Day has his workshop on the waterfront in Seattle. He does both commissions and spec pieces. This interior was designed and built for a client.

This page:
Additional views of an interior by Ross Day.

a second year. This second year amounts to a year of independent study; students have complete freedom to explore and challenge themselves in any way that is reasonable. We encourage visitors to our school to commission one of our second-year students to build a particular piece. This is a wonderful experience for the student, giving him or her a sense of reality and looking toward the future, but it is just as interesting for the person commissioning the piece because they can visit during the building; they can discuss the concept, the design, and then watch it evolve.

When working with clients, we encourage our second-year students to pay very close attention to the function of the piece, where it will be, how it will be used, what it should house, or any of the particulars that are important to the owner. The craftsman should respond to this with a few ideas and suggestions, and also with great respect to the wishes of the client. Thus the choice of craftsman is also the choice of a particular approach to workmanship.

These pieces live quite well in any home that represents a person or people with a balanced or fairly refined taste. Clients get what suits them and what they want to live with, rather than relying on period styles that may not suit their lives. An object that really suits one in every sense makes one happy; it is a joy to live with. So, a little freedom in choosing one's craftsman and approaching this whole matter of commission would certainly benefit many people, especially since by their nature the craftsmen who have been with us are not eccentric and publicity minded or showy in the sense of building anything for anyone. They give the potential client the chance to get a quiet, balanced, fine piece of workmanship.

Since most of our students past and present are living (and really feel good about living) a fairly balanced and modest life, they do not generally aspire to exorbitant prices and exclusiveness and an air of snobbishness about their work or their attitude or their relation to clients. It is all very friendly and quiet, and, we dare say, modest from the point of view of the craftsman, and thus the person asking for these services can feel quite secure in the honesty, integrity, and modesty of the craftsman.

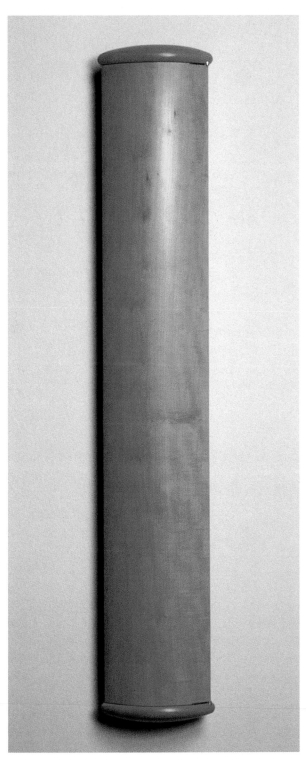

This page:
Aromatherapy cabinet, Richard Swift.
Pear wood. The door is shaped from a single
piece, thus eliminating the need for joinery in
this very demanding wood. Shelves are built in.
Richard came to the school from England,
where he now resides and works.
Life without industry is guilt; and industry
without art is brutality.

Ever since the beginning of the school, we have had annual student shows and even some special exhibitions that did not represent the entire year's work but were a select number of pieces shown in a gallery or elsewhere. We feel this is of tremendous importance as a form of encouragement to the students and to provide initial contact with the public. The response to the shows is a source of enjoyment and enrichment for the public as well.

This page:
"After Hours," a battery of drums designed, made, and used by Jefferson Shallenberger. Douglas fir.

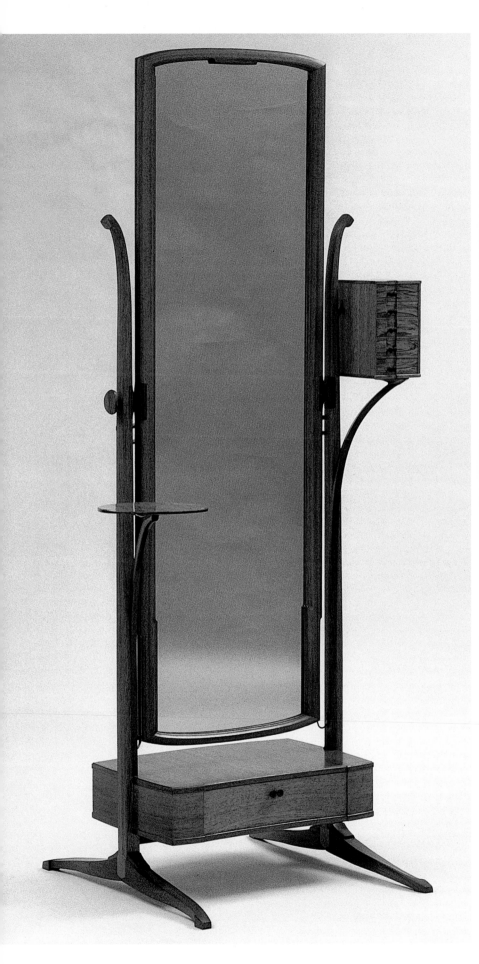

This page:
Dressing mirror, Ric Allison.
Kwila, yaka, pao ferro, Spanish
cedar. The angle is adjustable,
the drawer spaces convenient.
A complex and difficult piece, fault-
lessly done.

*"In this mirror, a focus was the ritual of
gathering adornments for enchant-
ment. A place was given for scarves, the
top of the posts for hats, the table for a
martini, pearls, lipstick, etc. The mirror
back reveals plumes of Pampas grass in
the grain."* —Ric Allison

Chairs

A very long time ago, when I was in school, I made a few chairs. They were designed by my professor, Carl Malmsten. Carl designed chairs for various purposes and occasions. Some were high style, while others were more casual. There were chairs especially intended for use with writing desks and chairs for other purposes. All were sensible in design, and suited to their purpose.

It occurred to me that Carl had designed some 150 chairs. Wegner, Mogensen, and the other Danes had designed very fine, world-famous chairs as well. In addition, there are thousands of architects and designers designing chairs. If each one of them had designed even 20 chairs, how many chairs have we got? Thinking in this way, the need to design yet another chair gradually left me. I just bypassed chair design and went on to cabinets, tables, and the like, and made those things my own.

This page and opposite:
Chair, Adrian Ferrazzutti.
Hickory and cowhide. A strong and elegant chair.

Even so, it would be unfair to say that all the good chairs have already been designed. Our students have made many sensible, comfortable, good-looking chairs. The chairs shown on these pages are some of the best.

As a chair-building exercise, I occasionally bring into the shop one of Malmsten's chairs from my home. We take the liberty of studying this well-made chair. A few people at the school have taken this study further, and made it an exercise in chair-making. This gives them the chance to experience a wonderful chair. They study the joinery and the angle of seating. They experience the comfort of the chair—the supple back piece and the crest rail which, though rather delicate, is not overdone.

My advice always is to simply calm down and make a good, comfortable chair. Do not compare it to others, or try to trace the origins. There are countless interpretations of the Windsor chair, the Shaker chair, the Peacock chair, and many other styles. So what? There will always be room in this world for at least one more comfortable, friendly, well-made chair.

This page:
Greenwood chairs, Dan Stalzer.
Above: Rocking chair, tanoak and cotton webbing.
Below: Chair, tanoak and hemp webbing.

"This style of chair is as old as the hills, and in fact that's where it comes from, the hills of Appalachia. Tanoak, an amazing wood native to Northern California lends itself to greenwood chairmaking techniques. The parts are shaped by hand while the wood is still green, using splitting tools and a drawknife. I use virgin wood, the fresher the better. It's as wet as a potato and almost as easy to shape. Friends have asked me to design 'my own' chair, and no doubt I will someday. But for now I'm happy to be making these ladderback chairs, and teaching others how to make them."

—Dan Stalzer

Opposite page:
Chaise lounge, Nick Clark.
Kwila and leather.
24 in. high, 84 in. wide, 48 in. deep.

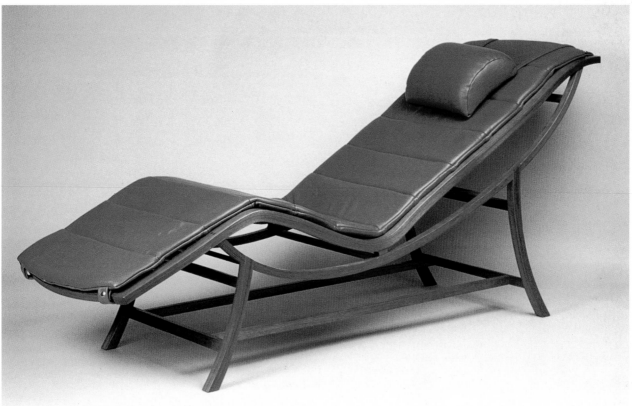

This page:

Above: Chairs, Michael Burns.
These chairs are reproductions of a chair designed by Vidar Malmsten around 1972.
Right: Chair, Kevin Greenlees.
Kwila. This is a faithful reproduction of a chair designed by Carl Malmsten in 1916. The original won a grand prize at the Stockholm City Hall, where it and others of its kind still stand. In an odd way, this event changed Malmsten's life: He became a designer instead of "just" a cabinet-maker.

Opposite page:

Above: Chair and footstool, Jason Hernandez.
Below: Sofa, Ross Day.

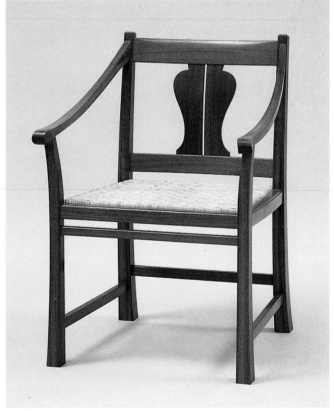

This page:

Above: Dining table and chairs, Ross Day.
Walnut with pear chair backs.

Right and below: Dressing table and stool, David Welter.

Kwila. This set is beautifully done. It was crafted while David was a student at the school. He is now an important staff member.

Opposite page:

Chinese chair, Yeung Chan.
This is a truly Chinese chair, faithful to the original in every respect. An amazing person, Yeung has the skill, historical knowledge, and reverence for this difficult work.

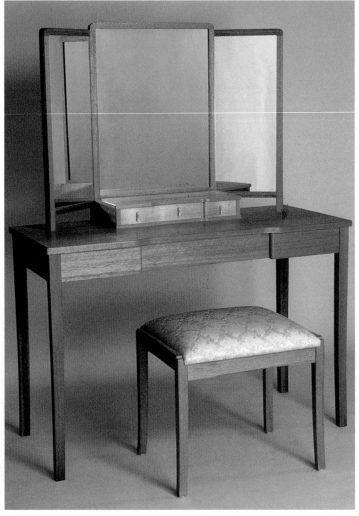

This page:
Chair, Joe Bush.

Opposite page:
Dining chair, David Kimball.
Claro walnut.

*My observation over 50 years is that the 'young'
continually find themselves in a free-for-all marketplace
fray. Why do they come to an old potter like me—unless
they have the hope that I hold a secret which they might
learn? I have no precious secret, only an humble
observation—namely, that if the desire for the good pot
and the vocation is strong enough and pure enough,
you can get there. Any sacrifice is worthwhile, including
life itself.*   *—David Leach*

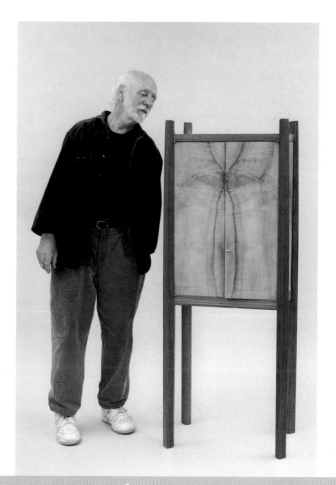

Section *3*: Wood

Start collecting. Get all the wood you can...
and then get some more!

Wood as Material

O f all the materials that people work with, wood is perhaps the one that is most alive. It is never static. Over the course of a few days, or years, or decades—even after a few centuries—it continues to move and subtly change dimension. Constantly reacting to changes in temperature and humidity, wood's changeable nature can make it a frustrating and challenging material to work with sometimes.

The very structure of wood—the way nature has composed and arranged the fibers—is part of the thrill and the charm of working it. Chemicals in the earth, as well as fungi and other living organisms that live on the wood itself, make each tree unique. Colors that come and go, and are sometimes so intense that one does not know what to do with them, are all part of wood's charm. To craftsmen like us, these things more than compensate for certain frustrations.

A weaver relates the type of fiber to the garment she is making. Thus woolen clothing is different from clothing made from Thai silk. You don't get the same inspiration from, nor do you use the same techniques when working with, radically different fibers, colors, and textures. So it is with wood.

Understanding the nature of a given type of wood, and the experience to know which tools and methods are most appropriate to working it, are what sets our kind of craftsman apart. Too many others neglect the subtleties of wood and pay too much attention to the sensationalism of color and design. To them, wood becomes secondary. It is not linked to their emotions and skills, or to the total concept of what the craftsman wants to do uncompromisingly. The craftsman should enjoy wood, be curious about it, and above all respect it.

The lines and patterns that the grain forms—the graphics of wood—have a tremendous effect. Indifference to the pattern value of the wood can produce a discordant effect. Experienced

Overleaf
Left: A piece of furniture begins to come to life. Right: Friendly, constructive comments rather than art-oriented critiques give students encouragement as well as food for thought.

This page and opposite:
Jewelry boxes, Paul Lynch. About 4.5 in. high, 15 in. long, 11 in. wide. Polish and wax finish. The box with the contoured lid (above) has walnut inserts. The lid with the carved grips (below) was made from a rare piece of pear wood. Notice the carefully spaced dovetails in both boxes. There should be rhythm in hand-done joinery, not simply rigid traces of a machine.

craftsmen know by looking at a plank how it should be cut to yield a surface that has a certain curve in the grain. They know how to get the color for a particular effect. The lines and rhythms and changes in color do matter. They mean the difference between a harmonious, beautiful piece of furniture and one that just sits. This difference is the result of awareness, deep caring, and an uncompromising attitude.

Much is being said about the depletion of forests and the ravaging of jungles and other places where precious trees grow. We relate very strongly to this situation, but we believe that the craftsmen who respect wood and wish not to misuse it are so few that they use but a tiny fraction of the wood that is being cut. We have connections with suppliers who are working with natives in the places where precious woods are being cut, and we try as much as possible to use these sources. We also have connections with general suppliers where one can find more common woods.

We have a young fellow from Canada who comes down with truckloads of western maple, some of it gorgeously quilted or spalted. I have a weakness (as do many of my students) for spalted wood, which is the work of nature. It's caused by fungus, and it's unpredictable. It often carries disappointments along with the magic. If the fungus has gone a little too far, the wood is unusable in furniture. There is a fine line between beauty and deterioration of the wood, and we try to walk it.

This page:
Above: Detail of spalted western maple from the cabinet below.
Below: "Posts" cabinet, James Krenov, 1998. The posts and rails are kwila, the horizontal veneered surfaces are spalted western maple. About 4 ft. 6 in. high. Polish and wax finish. The doors are unequal in size because a cut in any other location would have disturbed the pattern of the grain.

Opposite page:
Any cabinetmaker's envy. Wood stickered and stored in the best way possible.

Not long ago someone reminded me of something I said years ago, "Get wood. Get all you can, and then get some more."

We find treasures, sometimes locally. We even saw a log now and then. We have a Sperber chainsaw mill with two engines that we use to flitch-cut the few logs that are given to us or that we happen to come by.

But by and large we are simply the users of woods, hard and soft, where we can find them. We have a few suppliers we rely on, and we keep a small but good selection of wood for our students.

Among the common woods there may be something that is very valuable to a particular person who has an idea that circles around the colors, shades, and properties of a particular wood. There is a strong emotional connection between our kind of craftsman and all kinds of wood, so we try to obtain woods that will inspire our students. A good selection to choose from encourages them to explore further and learn more—to weave together ideas and inspirations with the colors, patterns and peculiarities of particular woods that we find.

The search for wood is the beginning of our kind of craftsman's existence. Certainly without wood a craftsman cannot work. It's important to have fine wood—interesting wood poses possibilities and sets the imagination in motion. Without that depth of feeling, the craftsman cannot achieve the inspiration and the refinement that we wish to emphasize in the work shown in this book.

It is not uncommon for clients to approach a craftsman and say, "I want this object made out of fir or pine, but I want it to look like mahogany." If someone wants a wood that looks like mahogany, we suggest mahogany itself, carefully selected. Many things now old were given color with the aid of stain, chemicals, and other techniques, and doing so is still the practice in some circles. We do not lean in that direction.

Another thing that is important in our relationship to wood is a knowledge of how wood reacts over time. There will be color changes. Most of these are predictable, some are very subtle, and not all of them are pleasing. Some woods age gracefully toward warm colors, while others lose color or change color in a way that is less attractive than the original color of the wood when it was newly surfaced. Mahogany ages quietly and rather beautifully, especially if it is fine mahogany and has the proper finish. Maple darkens a little with time and moves toward a yellow color. Douglas fir becomes richer, more reddish, and more mellow. Domestic American cherry is bound to become more red over the years, whereas European cherry usually retains its warm honey color. There are woods that lose color in daylight and exposure to air. The rosewood family pales a little bit in the course of time. Walnut tends to fade over the years. Certain tropical woods do the same.

These are all natural changes that the craftsman should be aware of. He or she should assume the responsibility of predicting, and even explaining, to the potential client or gallery, the changes that will occur in the wood used for any given piece. Thus if someone commissions a piece or sees something in a gallery, he or she will be made aware of what exposure to light and air will do. We don't want someone to be unhappy later on when the piece loses its color or becomes much darker than anticipated. When the changes have been predicted and talked about, they become satisfying. Doing this is part of the craftsman's caring, and a part of the way that he or she can communicate with the person who will live with the piece. It adds to the mutual experience.

Opposite page:
Showcase cabinet, Yeung Chan.
Kwila and mildly spalted western maple. 62 in. high, 21 in. wide, 16 in. deep. Shellac, polish, and wax finish. This cabinet will age gracefully since both woods are stable in color.

This page:
Tapered cabinet, Rita Martinez.
Vertical-grain Douglas fir, Port Orford cedar, and plum. 37 in. high, 17 in. wide, 12 in. deep.

This page:

Low cabinet, Ben Brungs. Eastern walnut. 40 in. high.

This cabinet has a sturdy but not strict look. The balance of proportions and curves is pleasing.

Opposite page:

Above: Detail of a piece by Michael Carroll.

The swirls and rhythm of grain have a lot to say about whether or not a piece sings.

Lower right: Chest of drawers, Seth Janofsky.

Red oak and common pine. 40 in. high, 36 in. wide, 20 in. deep. The use of common pine, brought to a high polish, was not used as a reference to rustic woodwork, but because it provided a patterned surface incorporating an element of natural irregularity.

Lower left: Cabinet, Michael Burns.

Color variations also occur in certain kinds of wood where nature has chemically given the tree different colors in its parts.

Some woods have a light surface with a darker pattern in the central area, other woods have the opposite. These variations in color are graphic aspects of the wood and need to be considered when designing and building the piece.

Craftsmen pay attention to these kinds of details because they do matter. We find that people react positively to these nuances. They may not know why, but they'll say things like, "I enjoy the feel of that piece; it has a special air about it." It does not have to be a rare piece of wood to have this special quality. Even an ordinary piece of pine can have a special quality if it is handled with care.

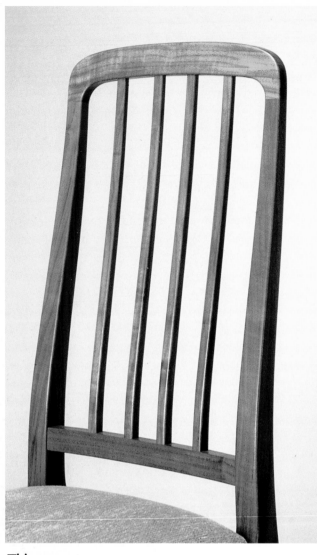

This page:

Above: Chair detail, Jim Budlong.
Claro walnut. Oil finish.
Right: Cabinet, James Krenov.
Teak. The plank curved, and it led to the design of
the stand. The door panels are lightly spalted
maple. The drawer fronts are olive.

Opposite page:

Dining table, Jim Budlong.
Claro walnut. 29.5 in. high, 82 in. long,
52 in. wide. Rubbed oil finish. Fine lines, flawless
workmanship. The piece has an almost delicate feel,
even though it is not small.

As David Pye, a wise man and professor at the Academy of Arts and Crafts in London, put it "The difference between the thing that sings and the thing that is forever silent is sometimes very small indeed." The difference between really caring and being a bit too casual in one's approach can deprive the object of the music that might have been within it.

A chair with a beautiful crest rail where the grain follows the curve of the back in a harmonious curve is sawn from a heavier, thicker piece. It was sawn with close attention to the annual rings and the way the grain ran through the wood. One can, with experience and patience, select pieces of wood where the grain is such that a certain cut will produce a given curve. The resulting grain pattern works with and enhances the shape of the piece.

These rhythms—lines that lift or support as opposed to those that are tired and sag—are things that may be taken for granted by the viewer who is not trained to see such details. They are neglected by the "time is money" or "I want to get it done quickly" craftsman. Are they important? Yes. Once one starts caring, they are important. This same principle applies to the other curved parts of a chair, for example in the arms and legs.

This grain pattern is also important in the stand of a cabinet that contains curves. Another illustration is the surface of a table. The grain of an oval table can accentuate the softness of the shape. Carelessly used, the grain will contradict the shape and there will be disharmony. Although the top is an oval, it will seem to have corners. Conversely, a rectangular table top or other surface can be made more friendly by choosing the grain so that it softens the rectangle. The corners are no longer aggressive, and there is a quiet wholeness about the shape. With carefully chosen grain, you don't have the feeling that you must avoid the corners because they are sharp to the eye. Sitting at that table, or approaching it, you feel welcome.

This page:
Credenza, Nick Clark.
Honduran mahogany, steamed European beech, granadillo, and maple. Veneered on a solid wood base. 33 in. high, 40.5 in. wide, 33 in. deep.

Opposite page:
Above: Low display cabinet, Seth Janofsky.
Black walnut and Port Orford cedar.
20 in. high, 56 in. wide, 16.5 in. deep. A single small knothole in the top creates an element of balanced symmetry and, in the right conditions, allows a shaft of sunlight to fall inside the cabinet.
Below: Sideboard, Joe Bush.
Black acacia, chechen, and mahogany.
Veneered carcase and solid doors. 34.5 in. high, 59 in. wide, 18 in. deep. Oil finish.

This page:

Above: Small display cabinet, Greg "Barney" Smith. Pear wood. About 18 in. high. Polished and waxed finish. Note how the details are crisply defined yet have a friendly feel.

"Forever onward and upward." —*Duke Ellington*

Right: Bow front cabinet, John Cameron. Hickory and ash, veneered. 60 in. high, 28 in. wide, 16.5 deep. Polish and wax finish.

This page:
Left: Buffet table,
Tim Patterson. Oak and spalted maple. 40 in. high, 35 in. wide, 14 in. deep.
Below: Sideboard, Erik Owen. European olive and ash. 34 in. high, 43 in. wide, 15.5 in. deep. The wood is very mild in texture and color; quite unlike the more common coarser ash found in the U.S. The decorative sprigs are inlaid.

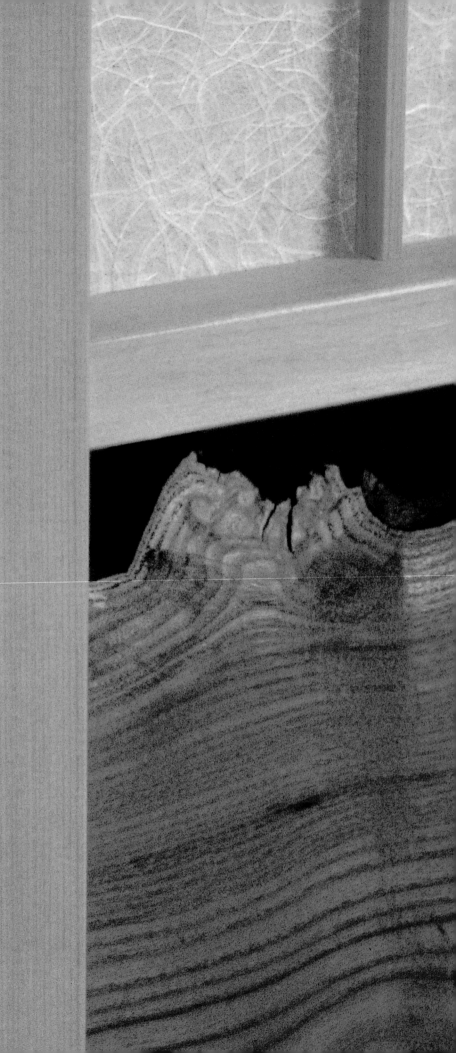

Grain

Overleaf:
Screen, Michael Carroll.
Port Orford cedar, mulberry, old growth cedar.

Opposite page:
Humidor, Les Cizek.
Wild tamarind. 10 in. high, 16 in. wide,
10 in. deep.

"The plank was a gift from a friend in Key West. The bottom part of it had amazing grain, and there was just enough to make the diamond pattern on the lid."
—Les Cizek

This page:
Blanket chest, David Fleming.
Eastern walnut, maple, and camphor. 26 in. high, 38 in. wide, 18 in. deep. Made from a single plank of walnut.

"Jim talks a lot about 'tension' in design, by which I think he means that there are few things in life as dull as a straight line. But put just a little strain on that line—give it a slight asymmetrical arc—and it becomes a whole other creature. Even one such subtle line can have a powerful effect."
—David Fleming

This page:
No-glass display cabinet, Gary Rawlins.
English brown oak, spalted maple, and
kwila. 58 in. high, 32 in. wide, 12 in.
deep.

*"Life is what happens while you're busy making
other plans."*

—*John Lennon*

This page:
Wall cabinet, Greg Zall.
Beech and spalted maple.
22 in. high, 12 in. wide, 6 in. deep.
Gentle curves, soft edges, with the
woods' patterns and grains
carefully arranged to harmonize.
Deceptively simple.

This page:

"Walkabout," Kevin Greenlees.
Kwila, with gently spalted maple panels, stand in wenge. About 4 ft. 6 in. high, 22 in. wide, 13 in. deep. From an original idea and a sketch, this piece evolved through a lot of searching. There were many variations—triangles paired rather than squares, strong contrast between light and dark wood, and glass in some openings. Originally from England, Kevin now lives in Fort Bragg.

This page:
Showcase, Konrad Horsch. Posts and framework of cherry, panels and drawer fronts of spalted maple. 60 in. high, 18 in. wide, 12 in. deep. The idea for this type of showcase is not new, but it is executed here with great clarity by Konrad, who came to us from Germany. The upper part is glassed in, and there are two delicately fitted doors on the ends. The three drawers slide smoothly on wood rails.

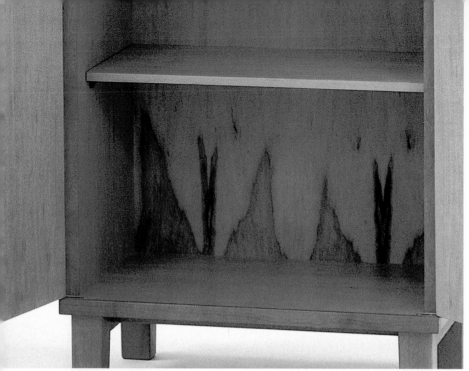

This page:
Port cabinet, Ashley Eriksmoen.
Claro walnut with inserts of lilac. 13 in. high,
5.5 in. wide, 5 in. deep.

"Certain spaces invite our imagination, allowing us to mentally project ourselves into that space, entering into a fantastic realm. As small interiors and details capture our attention, the full-scale world in our peripheral vision falls away."

—*Ashley Eriksmoen*

Marquetry

Over the years, our school has come to be known for the quality of the marquetry created by our students. Julie Godfrey wrote this essay while a student at The College of the Redwoods.

As I learned the art of cabinetmaking, I've had to develop skills that didn't come naturally to me—things like strict discipline, a slowing of pace, orderliness of thought, and a methodical work process. To me, marquetry offers a counterpoint to the sharp discipline of cabinetmaking. This contradicts most people's image of marquetry. When they see the large number of small, intricately fit pieces that marquetry involves, "freedom" is not a word that springs to mind. In marquetry I find the freedom to "paint" organic forms with a palette of woods. This offers a welcome measure of spontaneity and freedom to the making of furniture.

I was fortunate to learn the basics of the art of marquetry from fellow students at The College of the Redwoods in an environment where balance and harmony set the boundaries for design. Marquetry is not an art reserved only for those who consider themselves artists. I think anyone can develop enough skill in drawing to achieve a pleasing design with accurate perspective, shading, and line. As in cabinetmaking, it takes practice to develop skills of hand and eye.

The key to good marquetry is finding a balance between the image and the piece of furniture so they work together and even appear to need one another. All the various elements should reflect a common mood that gives the piece balance and harmony. These elements include the marquetry itself, wood choices, and grain patterns as well as the lines of the cabinet and the relationship to the negative space. The shape of the cabinet is every bit as important as the marquetry itself. Even the finest marquetry will not redeem an awkwardly

This page and opposite:
Petite cabinet, Julie Godfrey. Pear wood and moabi, rosewood stand. 56 in. high, 16 in. wide, 14 in. deep. Polished and waxed.

This page:

Small chest, Brian Condran.
15 in. high, 9 in. wide, 7 in. deep. A minor miracle, truly originating from the wood; flatsawn pieces of cocobolo that included both the typical reddish-brown heartwood and the very light sapwood. The base is machichi. Nature's work, treated with great respect.

"Will this take a long time to learn? Only a lifetime, my son, but perhaps a bit longer."
— *Quai-Chang Cain*

Opposite page:

Flower cabinet, Seth Janofsky.
White oak, red oak, and walnut. 30 in. high, 44 in. wide, 16 in. deep.

designed cabinet, and will look more like wallpaper than an integral part of the piece.

When starting a marquetry piece, I work from a finished drawing so that the whole composition has been considered. I draw from life or from photographs. I try to trust my eye about how objects actually appear in space instead of relying on my imagination. Without looking closely at a vase of flowers, we miss how the waterline distorts the stems. We must learn these things by actually seeing them. I try to make sure the perspective in my drawing is accurate and that the shading clearly indicates a consistent source of light. If the drawing is done well, I know that later on I can trust my lines, and the placement of various objects in the overall design as I am cutting.

Still sticking to my drawing, I then make general decisions about wood choices for every element in the design. This process gives me a basic idea of balance and how the colors will offset each other. I've learned that marquetry is most effective on either a very light or very dark background. Outside edges that are highlighted with a very fine white or black line can create a stunning effect that brings the form alive in three dimensions.

There is a remarkable range of color available naturally, and I take pleasure in being able to say that nature alone produces the rainbows in my work. I divide all my veneers into four tonal groups—whites, yellows, browns, and reds. Dyed woods are common in traditional marquetry, but I try to limit them as much as possible. The shading of a given object might require five to seven veneers within a tonal range.

The transition of tones from light to dark, while gradual, is rarely uniform. If I established clear shading in my original pencil drawing, then I know where the transition to darker tones should occur in order to create the desired effect.

Sometimes the use of wood grain alone can lend texture to a design. For this reason, I also set aside a fifth group of veneers with distinctive textures or grain patterns. Lacewood rays can simulate the scales of a fish, Macassar ebony streaks seem like bark on a tree trunk, and gumwood can look like the wrinkles in a face. Brass or shell can also be inlaid to simulate objects or simply add an exquisite visual element. It is also important to think about how wood tones will age, and how those altered tones will relate to each other over time. A well-planned marquetry cabinet will be appreciated by future generations.

As in the building of any piece of furniture, there is always an element of spontaneity. Final decisions about wood choices and grain patterns are often made as you go. You never know how successful the result will be until all the pieces have been cut and the finished panel is removed from the press. There are always surprises, and many elaborate marquetry works will continue to reveal details that first went unnoticed.

The possibilities for combining marquetry with furniture design are endless. A single, delicate stem of bamboo climbing across the front of a cabinet can be more impressive and effective than an elaborate landscape covering the entire surface. It is the lines, color, and grain pattern of a particular cabinet that will suggest the correct balance. The woodworker who lets these things guide the mood and the balance will likely create a work pleasing to live with for years to come.
                                              —*Julie Godfrey*

This page:

"Dragonfly" jewelry cabinet, Craig Vandall Stevens.
20 in. high, 12 in. wide, 8 in. deep. Fiddleback western
maple and ziricote, abalone, gold mother of pearl.
Marquetry woods: granadillo, pao ferro, wenge, ziricote,
satinwood, and holly.

*"Iridescent fiddleback maple suggests a watery background
for the marquetry reeds and grasses. Inlaid dragonflies of abalone
and mother of pearl help complete the quiet scene of a summer
pond. Inside are nine ziricote dovetailed drawers with carved pulls. A
marquetry bee made of satinwood, ebony, and mother of pearl flies
across one of the drawers. The finish is shellac and beeswax."*
—*Craig Vandall Stevens*

This page:
"Falling Leaf" sideboard,
Brian Condran. 34 in. high, 38 in. wide,
18 in. deep. The tapered sides of this
quiet piece called for some inventive
fashioning of hinges.

This page:
Elliptical cabinet, Zivko Radenkov. Douglas fir, with frame and legs of Andaman padouk. Flowers of pink ivorywood. 4 ft. 3 in. high, 20 in. wide, 14 in. deep.

This rare elliptical cabinet should be in a museum. The shape is very difficult to balance; there is only one ideal position for the legs. Move them a bit, and the cabinet seems to tip.

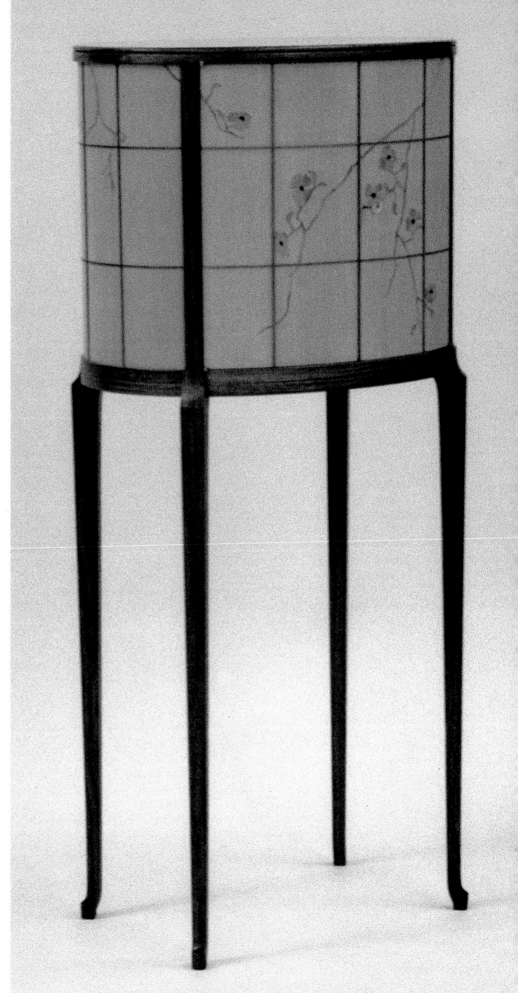

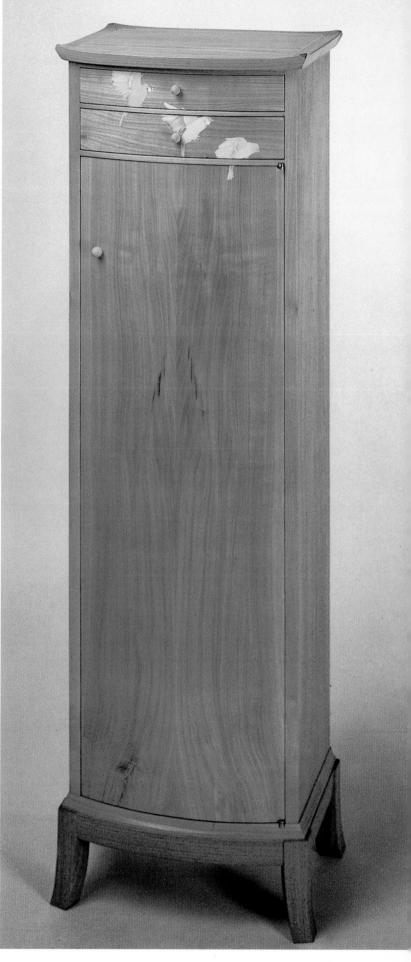

This page:
Above: "Rose" jewelry box, Brian Condran.
Mendocino cypress, rose made of African
pink ivory and bloodwood, leaves and stems
of poplar. 10 in. high, 8 in. wide, 7 in. deep.
Right: Cabinet, Greg Zall.
European cherry. 41 in. high, 13 in. wide,
10 in. deep.

This page:
"Sunflower" cabinet, Greg Zall.
Douglas fir reclaimed from a chicken hatchery, satinwood, ebony, and lignum vitae. 60 in. high, 34 in. wide, 20 in. deep.

This page:

"Chickadee" cabinet, Craig Vandall Stevens. Norway maple, white oak, kwila, beech, and lilac. Marquetry woods: bay laurel, ebony, holly, bubinga, alder, and doussie. 52 in. high, 25 in. wide, 17 in. deep. The individual pieces of marquetry are shaded with hot sand to create a sense of depth. Inside the cabinet there is a pair of curved-front kwila and beech drawers with hand-cut dovetails and a single adjustable shelf. The door pull is carved from lilac.

"I enjoy designing and making furniture that complements the decorative art of marquetry. What I had in mind was a cabinet with subtle curves and a delicate presence that could become the canvas for a picture in wood. The subtle greens and reds of the Norway maple create the feeling of a watercolor wash behind the design. White oak for the legs and rails provides a framework for the picture."

—Craig Vandall Stevens

Parquet

This page and opposite:
Parquet cabinet, Dan Grenier.
Norway maple. Surprisingly, the parquet pattern is made of just one wood with strong prismatic characteristics.

A t its best, marquetry is an orderly pursuit that involves graphic art and careful work. Parquetry, on the other hand, requires a portion of skill, a bit of intuition, and a great deal of luck.

The luck starts with finding the wood. One of the best sources are those odds and ends of wood that many people think are not good for much. Curious craftsmen are attracted to such wood—it is a puzzle waiting to be solved. Some of the most interesting parquet work originates with a short plank cut from the base or crotch of a log where the grain is all aswirl with colors.

No matter what play the grain has, some species of wood are better suited to parquet work than others. Those are the woods that have the quality of refraction—not just in the grain, but in the very cells. This gives those woods a satin-like appearance. To understand what I mean, resaw a piece of maple and lay the pieces together bookmatched. Each side catches the light differently than the other—one side appears lighter than the other. Reverse the pieces and the effect remains. This cellular play in wood can be bothersome, causing an unwanted striped effect in a tabletop or door panels.

But it can be most suitable in parquetry. Using only one species of wood, you can create a variety of geometric patterns on a piece of furniture. You can create an orderly pattern—as in a brick wall or parquet floor—and the resulting surface is interesting but quiet. Or you can follow another road. This starts with the piece of wood itself, with its own particular swirls of grain and streaks of color.

Some years ago, I made a doodle sketch of a two-part cabinet. It lay almost forgotten until I met a very generous fellow from whom I was able to beg a small plank of English walnut, the only piece he had. It came from the butt end of a log, from near the roots. The grain was very steep in some places,

and flat in others. The piece had lively colors in swirls and curves. This wood said, "Veneer!" and I listened. That old sketch came to mind, and I knew that at last I had the wood I needed to build something.

Sawing the veneer, I was happy. All sorts of images tumbled in my head. School was out, so there was plenty of space in the shop. I spread the veneers on the floor and climbed the workbenches to peer hopefully down at my selections. Then I'd descend to the floor, rearrange the pieces, and climb up again for another look. Very slowly the parts started to come together. It actually felt like I knew what I was doing. And yet, when the cabinet was done, I realized that it was better than I can do. Stanley Doubtfire (page 12) would understand.

This page and opposite:
Parquet cabinet, James
Krenov. English walnut. 5 ft.
3 in. high, 21 in wide, 13 in.
deep. Polish and wax finish.
Made in 1994.

This page:

Cabinet on stand, Vajra Rich.
English white oak, kwila, pine. Shellac, polish, and Clapham's wax finish. Notice the subtle yet effective use of oak pieces that contain some of the much lighter sapwood.

Opposite page:

Post and panel cabinet with open show space, Jason Hernandez. Careful use of shades and lines help enliven the large surfaces of this piece.

This page and opposite:
"Fat Boy," J. P. Vilkman, of Finland. Mahogany, ebony, maple Spanish cedar, wenge, and machiche. 5 ft. 6 in. high, 5 ft. long, 18 in. deep. This large 3-part cabinet is made from an oddly textured mahogany. Old-fashioned, but not out of date.

The difference between the thing which sings and the thing which is forever silent is often very slight indeed. Why should one feel impelled to go on trying to make something which sings I really do not know, but that apparently is the fate of artists in however small a field. Perhaps in the end we do it in the hope that in time to come someone's eye will light when they see a thing we have made and they too will feel the same impulse. Perhaps all good art has been addressed to a generation still unborn. —David Pye

Section 4: Creativity

· The Creative Process

· Emotions of Creation

There is no need to assert your mastery over the piece.
Let the design unfold as you work, be flexible,
and open yourself to what it will say as the work progresses.

The Creative Process

Time does not allow us to teach design and drawing as subjects. After all, people want to make shavings and build things. We have developed ways of composing pieces from a doodle or a rough sketch. We would not prevent anyone from making a drawing, but we would question if the final object needs to follow that drawing exactly. Sometimes the first sketch, done from way down deep somewhere, is what ends up being built. More often, things are designed by taking one step forward, one step back. Then we mock it up, and look at it closely, imagining the graphics of the piece. We want students to go slowly enough to pay attention to the emotional side, and leave options for discovery.

We avoid letting students reach the point of no return. It would be terrible if the student got to a point where nothing was going to work well. We would all suffer then. As instructors we always try to keep the student on track—one step ahead and a little step back, then turn around and look at the piece another way.

It's important that you first determine the proper sequence of work. Determine in your mind what the most important aspect of the piece is, and think about what can go wrong. You are better off doing the most difficult parts first, because if something goes wrong there, everything has been spoiled. Use your own logic and don't rely on traditional ways of looking at things. Gradually your judgement improves.

A part of the process is learning to deal with mistakes. Many mistakes are only temporary difficulties. Most of the time there is a way around difficulties that does not compromise either the piece or the craftsman's integrity. It is possible to fix most mistakes in a way that leaves you honestly happy. Doing so is an important part of the craftsman's honest work.

We try to work with students to make sure they are building things that feel right. We want them

Overleaf:
Left: Students help each other crosscut a plank with a bowsaw.
Right: Patrick Stafford contemplates the next step in the making of his two-piece cabinet of claro walnut.

This page:
A child's toy figure ascends a ladder to a mock-up within a mock-up.

Opposite page:
Developing an idea at the bench-cum-drawing table.

This page:

Cabinet, Om Anand. Monterey cypress. 13 in. high, 9 in. wide, 6 in. deep. Genuine naiveté is not common. We see a great deal of by-the-roadside handmade, the relaxed whimsical, and other variations on less-than-perfect. The composition of this cabinet and shelf represents Om as he is: meditative, gentle, and sincere.

Opposite page:

Secretaire, Austin Meinert. Douglas fir. How will it look? Austin used our big chalkboard to develop his idea. (See page 14 for a close up.)

to be happy building a piece because it comes close to the limitations of their skills. We don't want them to be intimidated by doing the work, nor do we want them to feel immobilized by the attempt. I suppose there is some pressure on students. There seems to be this self-defeating notion that the other students are doing all this advanced work. It's not always true. Some of the loveliest things made at the school have been lovely because of their simplicity.

There's a difference between what some people call whimsical or folksy and a piece that is genuinely naivé. It is a quality that can't be imitated. In one of my slide shows, I display a piece made by a student that shows a genuine naiveté. It is a little cabinet with a shelf for a small Buddha. The shelf was a plank, the cabinet opened and closed, and there was a drawer you could maneuver in and out. It had real charm and that is why I include it along with the more disciplined things that come from our shop. This piece is relaxed, not an uptight, highly disciplined piece standing at attention and never smiling. This piece smiles. There's a natural quality that some people have—they make things that are friendly.

When designing and building a functional object, your first step is to put yourself in the posi-

tion of the user. What will make this piece comfortable and enjoyable to live with? What sort of features does it need to make it comfortable in its intended function?

If the object is purely decorative, your responsibility changes. Sometimes the main functions are to be beautiful, to appeal to the senses, and to convey the intimacy of the process involved in making it. At other times, the focus can be to amuse and delight by creating something with an element of discovery, or to make an object that simply calls out to be played with.

Bob Dylan sang "The times they are a-changin'...." So true. Of late there has been a movement toward something called "Studio Furniture." We thought we had a shop, or workshop. But no—that has to change. Ours is a *Studio* now.

So, we get with it. Does this mean the work we do, and want to do, will be better—or only more pretentious?

Back to design: When you have sketched your concept and selected the wood, you can draw the characteristics and rhythms of that piece of wood on your sketch to see how they work visually. See what kinds of graphic lines the grain of the wood will give you. You must become sensitive to the lines, arches, and swirls of the grain and how they

work with the shape of the piece. In all your pieces you should strive for beautiful lines.

The best way to get lines that have life is to draw them freehand. Such lines have a dynamic tension, a subtlety that can only be achieved though sensitivity and a trained sense of rhythm

When you have established a design to work with, the next step is to make a rough mock-up. This is done to scale using cardboard and scrap. The point here is not to work out details, but to see the design in three dimensions. This will reveal aspects of a piece that can't be discerned from a drawing. In the mock up we can see things like the volume of space beneath a table that is created and contained by its legs. The mock-up lets you know whether the piece has balance or if it's a bit off. You can take this mock-up one step further by drawing in lines to represent the grain and adding some shading around certain construction elements.

Just looking at a simplified mock-up can set your fantasy going. If that happens, it becomes very important to know where and when to look ahead—what to leave for shaping later, and when the time comes to fill in the details.

There are many elements in play at this stage of design. You have to learn to do a number of things in combination. Knowing when to do something, controlling your fantasy, letting yourself read the wood, changing your mind, and letting the piece grow are all part of this process of composing. In the long run, if you're going to establish yourself as an individual craftsman, this is an essential skill to learn.

There is no need to assert your mastery over the piece. Let the design unfold as you work, be flexible, and open yourself to what it will say as the work progresses.

This page:

Perhaps the most important benefit of mock-ups is that they give a sense of volume; the true size of the intended piece. This is difficult to see in a drawing. Some details can be added to the mock-up, but others will only emerge after the wood is chosen and the piece develops.

Opposite page:

Les Cizek watches a discarded mock-up turn to smoke and ashes in the evening air.

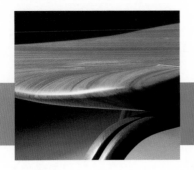

Emotions of Creation

Skills without emotion are mere mechanics. Every piece we do here evolves from both feelings and skills. We live in curves. We can get into patterns and shapes that evolve from the work we've done and seen, but there is always room for experiment, room for asking ourselves a lot more questions as we begin a project. It is essential to get off to a start that gives you energy rather than draining your resources.

You've got to go for what really attracts you, and this attraction and sense of possibility are personal matters. You've got to leave room to imagine what you can do. Should this be a little thinner, should it curve a little bit, should it be straight? Test options and experiment at the beginning, and even up to the first clamp-up. and see what you've put together.

All along ask if you're very pleased or just sort of pleased. You want the piece to boost your energy level and your optimism. I'm not saying you must be ecstatic about it, but every little bit helps. You don't want to get bogged down.

There is a lot of frustration until you decide what you really want to do. And that bears on your skills. The intimacy or flexibility of skills is the final criteria, not the mechanics. Some of us walk around checking everything with straightedges and squares, but knowing when square can be a little bit off is even better. You have two legs and they are parallel but they seem to converge, so you take a little tiny bit off the top of each one, just two shavings, and they open up just a fraction and the thing comes to rest visually.

That kind of flexibility is a great thing. Your materials become more malleable. You can work them, give them little changes along the way. Square has to be square when you're doing drawers, but square doesn't have to be square when you're doing a stand unless you want it to be. It might be better a little bit unsquare. You will grad-

Opposite page:
"Quarrel" loveseat, Ashley Eriksmoen.
Canary wood and welded steel.

"This seat not only dictates the position of the two quarrelers, it is a manifestation of the quarrel itself. As with all things in nature, the seats are not quite symmetrical and not quite identical. While my work tends to be very conceptual, it is important to me that it is well crafted. This piece is not something I could just knock out on a machine. In making it, I relied heavily on the hand skills that I aquired at The College of the Redwoods."
—*Ashley Eriksmoen*

ually discover that it is just a line, that you can make it look this way, that way, or some other way.

The start of any piece is very important. If you go off on one tack and then lose steam because the wood or something else disappoints you, you start working against yourself. You realize all at once that your heart isn't in it. Not for romantic reasons, but for very concrete ones. You chose that wood and it is not doing anything for you. No matter how you turn it, it is not what you thought it was going to be. You've got to get to a start that gives you energy rather than drains your energy.

A reputation may give you freedom. You gain not notoriety, but stability. People come to you and want you to do certain things. They won't tell you how it should look, they realize that you are on a level where you should have your say about the design. This will come surprisingly soon. You will have the chance to exercise your flexibility, your freedom, and your input into the things they want. You will also be able to make pieces even when no one is waiting for them. You can say to yourself, "I'm going to make this and it is going to be irresistible. People will line up to get it." That is what we strive for.

This page and opposite:
Cabinet, Adrian Ferrazzutti. Guatambu, katalox, and yellow cedar. 60 in. high, 21.75 in. wide, 11.5 in. deep. Talent, when we encounter it, can be uplifting. It widens the horizon and stimulates the teacher. It tends to encourage and excite the students. Adrian made a chair that was all handsome curves. Then he made this cabinet, which is all straight lines. We called it "The Mondrian Piece."

It seems to me like this. It's not a terrible thing — I mean it may be terrible, but it's not damaging, it's not poisoning to do without something one really wants....What's terrible is to pretend that the second-rate is first rate. To pretend that you don't need love when you do; or you like your work when you know quite well you're capable of better.

—Doris Lessing

Section 5: Fingerprints

· Leave Fingerprints

· Details

*The understanding eye sees the maker's
fingerprints. They are evident in every detail....*

Leave Fingerprints

In his wonderful book *The Unknown Craftsman*, Yanagi (through his translator, Bernard Leach), tells us that we should not be overly analytical in our observation of crafts. We needn't use mathematics, proportional drawings, weights, or measures to explain exactly why a piece of craftwork is pleasing. There is no need to trace the derivation of the piece or name the styles that informed the design. Yanagi says that all we must do is engage the piece with our feelings and intuition. We must perceive the work, not merely observe it.

When we truly perceive a piece of furniture, we take it in using all our senses. When we open ourselves to the piece, it becomes a person-to-person experience. We connect with the maker at precisely the level of effort and talent that he or she put into the process of conceiving and making the object.

Overleaf:

Left: Shaping the mouth of a plane to a pleasing curve won't make the tool any more effective, but it will enhance the experience of the craftsman.
Right: The plane produces a perfect paring.

This page and opposite:

Guitar, Jack Bogdanovich.
This guitar changed the maker's life. A good cabinetmaker when he came to us, Jack spent a year honing his skills. Then, suddenly, he was unsure. A talented musician, he was drawn to guitars. We were able to squeeze him in for a second year; he built a truly fine instrument. Jack is now acknowledged as a maker of exquisite classical guitars.

This page and opposite:
Altar, Myrick Ashley.
Cherry, tambooti, and alligator juniper.

"This piece was commissioned by Lobsang P. Lhalungpa, a revered Buddhist scholar, translator, and teacher. Lhalungpa knew that he wanted the cabinet to have two side drawers and a glass front and top, but the rest he left up to me. The piece, which I worked on for a year on and off, was a labor of love. I have a note from him telling me that the cabinet had been consecrated."

—Myrick Ashley

This page:
Right: Music stand, Darragh Perrow.
Polished mahogany.
Below: Anniversary box, Cameron Schiff.
10 in. high, 20 in. wide, 15 in. deep. Mendocino
cypress and black acacia.

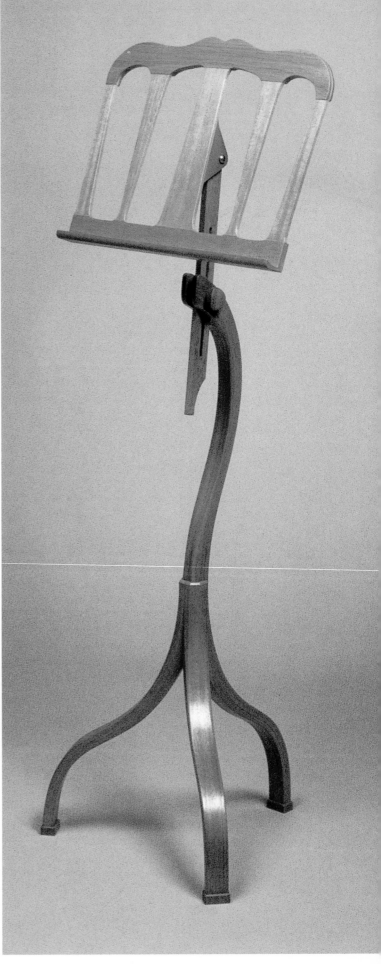

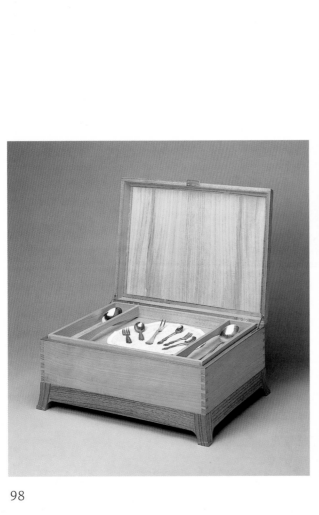

This page:
Above: Reliquary box, Om Anand. Monterey cypress and kwilla.

Below: "Chili Pepper Tea Cabinet," Michael Prendergast. English elm and spalted maple. 25 in. high, 16 in. wide, 7 in. deep. The back panel detail is elm, wenge, and lambskin. The screens are done with homemade Japanese paper.

This page:
"Slacken Pair," cocktail tables, Ric Allison.
Macassar and Gabon ebonies, grenadillo. Tapered bent laminated legs, compound coopered tops.
Shellac, polish, and varnish finish. Ric is a superb craftsman and an innovative designer.

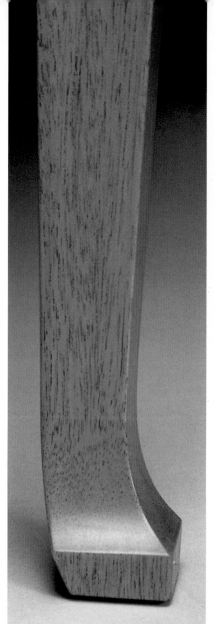

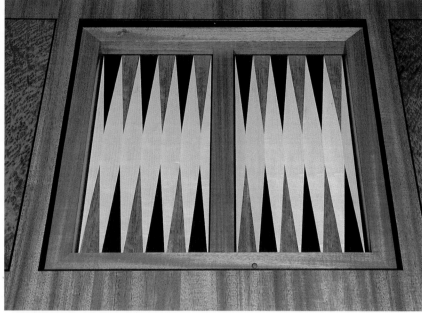

This page:

Game table, Ejler Hjorth-Westh. Mahogany, redwood burl, ebony, maple, bubinga, and wenge. 29 in. high, 53 in. long, 32 in. deep. The client brought a chessboard and asked for a "Queen Anne flavor" table to accommodate it and a backgammon board. Ejler came up with a table with straight lines accented by a few tight curves. The details are crisp, the symmetry calm.

Details

T he understanding eye sees the maker's fingerprints. Fingerprints are evident in every detail—the choice of the wood, the texture of the surfaces, the treatment of the edges, the joinery that is visible and invisible, the finish that has been used, how that finish was applied, and a thousand other things.

This page:
"Hide and Seek Curio Box," Ashley Eriksmoen. Pear parquetry exterior, camphor veneered and solid interior, maple dovetailed drawer. 5.5 in. high, 17 in. wide, 11 in. deep.

"To enliven an otherwise symmetrical piece, I created an irregular geometric pattern inspired by the ones on Moorish treasure chests. I made a puzzle-like top with parquetry tiles that slide on tongue and groove rails, allowing one to hunt for buried treasure. While making it, I thought of the box Jim built for King Gustav of Sweden to house his collection of stoneware miniatures, and the pleasure of keeping and arranging small treasures."

—Ashley Eriksmoen

Opposite page:
Box for precious objects, Reg Herndon. Kwila, oxidized copper. 6.5 in. high, 14 in. wide, 9 in. deep. This box has an appealing medieval look. Difficult to make, it proved to be well worth the effort. Reg is now studying furniture restoration in England.

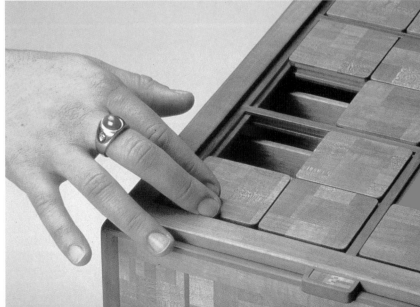

This page:
Hope chest, Ejler Hjorth-Westh.
Douglas fir, mahogany, and Port Orford
cedar. 19 in. high, 38 in. wide, 21 in.
deep. When a cold day in late fall makes
you think of a wool sweater, this is where
it will be. The fragrance of cedar and
wool blends with the soft light from a
weak sun. Altogether, it spells winter.

Opposite page:
Jeweler's tool box, Erik Owen.
Hickory box with pao ferro stand.
12 in. high, 20 in. wide, 8.5 in. deep.
Eric built this tool box to trade rent on
his cabin while going to The College of
the Redwoods.

This page:
Cabinet on a light, tall stand. James Krenov. Maple case, kwila stand. Case: 20 in. high, 18 in. wide, 9 in. deep. 1995. The panels in the door frames curve away in reference to a fondness for sailing.

This page:

Flower table, Yeung Chan. Difficult joinery and a sure eye. Yeung has great respect for all fine work in China: This is a faithful reproduction of a table that would typically be used to hold flowers.

This page:

"Well Read Book" cabinet on a stand, Margaret O'Brien. Mahogany, walnut, and Douglas fir, drawer handles and inlay of sterling silver. 54 in. high, 25 in. wide, 9.75 in. deep. Shellac, polish, and wax finish.

"The curve of the solid cabinet door is coopered and the flip at the bottom is carved. Jim Krenov said that the door reminded him of a falling leaf."

—Margaret O'Brien

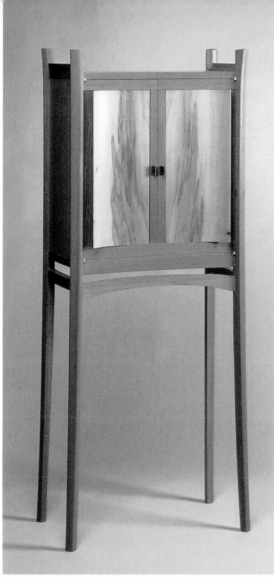

This page:
"Soaring," Charles Mantei. Pear and camarare.
59 in. high, 23.5 in.wide, 12.5 in. deep.

*"Originally my intention was to make this cabinet
larger, but Jim suggested that I shrink it down and make it more
personal. 'Make it so you can put your arms around it,' he said.
The legs are five sided, which adds a softness to the lines of the
piece. It took six tries to get them just right. Inspired by another
student who put secret compartments in all his work, I added
one in the side of this cabinet just for the fun of it."*
—Charles Mantei

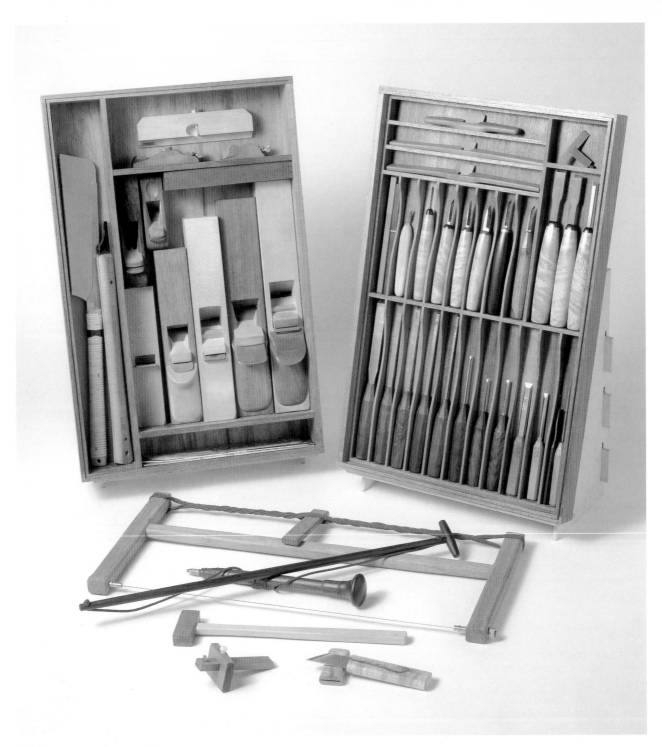

This page and opposite:

Tool box, Yeung Chan. Walnut. Yeung often travels around the country teaching and demonstrating. He built this box to transport his tools and hold them so they were easy to get to while working. The bottom photo at right shows how the cover for each half of the box can be assembled to make its stand. Yeung makes all of his hand tools, except saw blades and measuring tools.

"I love to make things with my hands. Grew up in a place lacking material, tools, and instructions. I had to find out the ways of how to do it and use material effectively. First the desire, then the idea, the plan, the method in mind followed by action. Sometimes mistakes and redone. With the mind, the eyes and hands work together, the dreams come true, the goal is achieved. Looking at the ceiling with two hands holding the chin doesn't do any good."

—*Yeung Chan*

Hardware

Since we build step-by-step and do mock-ups along the way, it is common for students to try different sizes, shapes, and placements of hardware. Eventually they arrive at something that leaves them satisfied that the work has achieved an interesting harmony.

There are practical matters to attend to. Doors need to be hung properly. Common butt hinges may be used, but in many instances these are rather awkward. We find that knife hinges mortised into the top and bottom of the door are much more discreet and certainly just as strong. They work very well and are remarkably strong given their size. When we have acute angles and curved parts, our students sometimes make their own knife hinges, which is quite an accomplishment in itself. They are neat and well done.

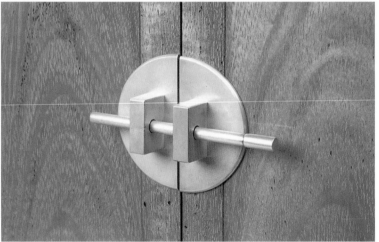

This page:
Above: "Little Tough Guy," Thea Gray.
Middle: Detail of pull, "Little Tough Guy."
Below: Hardware detail from a cabinet by Michael Burns.

This page:
Cabinet pulls, clockwise from upper left:
Cabinet by James Krenov, pulls by John Burt.
Cabinet by Michael Burns.
Cabinet by Bill Merikallio
Cabinet by Dan Curtis.
Cabinet by Darragh Perrow.

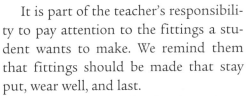

It is part of the teacher's responsibility to pay attention to the fittings a student wants to make. We remind them that fittings should be made that stay put, wear well, and last.

We try to convey that hardware is an integral part of the piece, not a mere decoration. It relates to how the piece is handled. It's important for our hand to feel comfortable as we open or close a door or a drawer. At some elevations our hands seems to feel more comfortable with a horizontal pull. At other elevations our arms just instinctively want to reach out for a vertical handle.

Careful attention to the fittings we use on our work is essential if we are to achieve harmony in the finished piece. The fittings must be not only comfortable to use, they must also be firmly set and sturdy. We don't want a pull or handle to break or come unglued. We think it very important that the things that we build will wear well and, of course, feel comfortable.

Opposite page:
Cabinet pulls, clockwise from upper left:
Cabinet by Bobby Watson.
Cabinet by Larry Riordan.
Cabinet by Yeung Chan.
Cabinet by Adrian Ferrazzutti.

This page:
Cabinet pulls, clockwise from upper left:
Cabinet by René Oschin.
Ccabinet by Michael Carroll.
Cabinet by Michael Prendergast.

Drawers

I was taught to make drawers that have a certain snugness. Drawers built that way don't rattle or bang, and they have a pleasant feeling when they slide. This is not something I invented. It isn't a completely different type of drawer—it's just an integral part of all good drawers everywhere.

I was able to convey this in my books, and I've found that people get a great deal of pleasure trying to get the same result in their own work.

This page:

Drawers by Nick Clark.

This page:
Clockwise from upper right:
Drawer by James Krenov.
Drawers by Seth Janofsky.
Drawer by Michael Carroll.
Drawers by Nick Clark.

Small tansu, Cindy Park.
This piece derives part of its
look from the wrought iron
pulls by John Burt.

This page:
Top: Drawer by Doug Chamblin.
Above and right: Small jewelry box,
Jennifer Anderson. Pear wood,
machiche, and maple.
13 in. high, 11 in. wide, 7 in. deep.
The challenges encountered in
building this box are belied by its
simple, clean look.

This page:
Box, Jefferson Shallenberger. Holly, mahogany, Alaska cedar, and narra. 44 in. high, 9 in. wide, 9 in. deep. Jeff wanted an element of mystery in this box, so made it difficult to distinguish drawers from panels. The solution to the mystery is to use a magnetic key as a pull.

This page:
"Komposition #7: Window into Broken Dreams,"
J. P. Vilkman. Yellowhart, bloodwood, verawood,
bayo, kwila, canarywood, black palm, ebony,
wenge, maple, and Spanish cedar. 55 in. high,
44 in. wide, 20 in. deep.

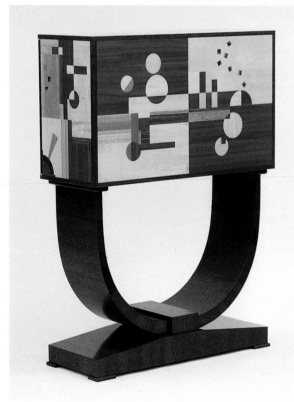

Afterword

Is there a conclusion to be drawn from this attempt at a book? Certainly a more learned person might draw one. It would include reflections on style, derivation, an attempt at judging quality—even an inevitable evaluation.

I leave that to others.

For me, there is only this: Many of the things shown here are precious objects. Furniture or not, regardless of the marketplace and career critics, the worth of such things is their whole content. Not to be analyzed or dissected, but to be seen. Seen—and lived with, in a coming together of sense and observation that will bring quiet joy long after the maker is forgotten

—James Krenov

Index of Makers

Photos by Seth Janofsky, except as noted below

Stuart Allan	38, 39
Damia Andrus	16
Cynthia Bodenhorst	8
Mark Johnston	88, 89
Anne Knudsen	117
Kitty Leaken	96, 97
Jay Odee	28
John Perrins	41
George Post	103
Mark Saffron	32
Kevin Shea	101
Jeff Shirley	69, 108
Sean Sprague	14, 84, 85, 104, 117, 132
Stephen Webster	66, 71
David Welter	covers, viii, 1, 7, 11, 18, 24, 25, 30, 35, 37, 44, 78, 81, 90, 93, 108

Editor: Aimé Fraser
Designer: Claudia Chapman
Managing Editor: Laura Tringali